PREVENTING BULLYING

HELPING KIDS FORM POSITIVE RELATIONSHIPS

Meline Kevorkian

Rowman & Littlefield Education
Lanham, Maryland • Toronto • Oxford
2006

Published in the United States of America
by Rowman & Littlefield Education
A Division of Rowman & Littlefield Publishers, Inc.
A wholly owned subsidiary of The Rowman & Littlefield Publishing Group, Inc.
4501 Forbes Boulevard, Suite 200, Lanham, Maryland 20706
www.rowmaneducation.com

PO Box 317
Oxford
OX2 9RU, UK

British Library Cataloguing in Publication Information Available

Library of Congress Cataloging-in-Publication Data

Kevorkian, Meline M., 1968–
  Preventing bullying : helping kids form positive relationships /
Meline M. Kevorkian.
    p. cm.
  ISBN-13: 978-1-57886-483-6 (hardcover : alk. paper)
  ISBN-10: 1-57886-483-6 (hardcover : alk. paper)
  ISBN-13: 978-1-57886-484-3 (pbk. : alk. paper)
  ISBN-10: 1-57886-484-4 (pbk. : alk. paper)
  1. Bullying in schools—Prevention. 2. School violence—Prevention. 3.
School children—Conduct of life. I. Title.
  LB3013.3.K48 2006
  371.5'8—dc22
                                    2006006813

∞™ The paper used in this publication meets the minimum requirements of
American National Standard for Information Sciences—Permanence of
Paper for Printed Library Materials, ANSI/NISO Z39.48-1992.
Manufactured in the United States of America.

CONTENTS

PREFACE

When you ask your child how his or her school day was and he or she bursts into tears over issues with friends or interactions with teachers, you are not alone. You can help your child gain positive interaction skills to build and maintain healthy relationships. This book contains eight rules to instill in your child to help them make friends and foster positive relationships. Each chapter contains real issues regarding relationships with peers, teachers, and adults. With each etiquette rule, you will find easy advice, practical tips, and examples to help you give your child the skills he or she needs to form healthy relationships.

INTRODUCTION

As I'm driving to school drilling my younger son on his spelling words, I'm listening to my older son talk about a classmate picking on him. At the same time, my two nieces who ride to school with us in the morning are telling me about how mean their friends are to them. Gianna, my four-year-old niece, repeats "Gianna Pianna, Gianna Pianna" and is whining about a boy in her class who always calls her bad names. Tatiana, my fourteen-year-old niece, is putting in her contacts, despite the fact her eyes are irritated, because she will be embarrassed if her "friends" see her in glasses. It doesn't matter that the designer glasses are new and cost my sister a small fortune. School mornings are often hectic just getting everyone fed, dressed, teeth brushed, and out the door on time without the added resistance of "this one hates me."

So in between spelling words I'm teaching Gianna an old-time favorite saying, "Sticks and stones can break my bones but names will never hurt me." Tatiana just chuckles and says, "Tell her the truth Auntie"; school days can sometimes be blue days. As an educator and writer who strives to give parents easy advice on how to help their children succeed in school, I decided I had to share the eight etiquette rules that can help children form relationships with parents, teachers, and other children that allow them to reach their potential in school and in life outside the classroom.

You may be wondering why relationships with others are so critical to school success. The older children get, the more important peer relationships become. Friends provide an opportunity for children to learn self-control, problem solving, and how to understand their emotions.

Many children today complain they have no friends and are unhappy the majority of their forty-hour school week. Research supports the belief that children must feel a sense of belonging and excitement at school in order to reach their potential. As a parent or teacher, you have heard the famous lines, "I have no friends" and "Everyone is mean to me." Peer rejection in childhood may have serious side effects such as low self-esteem and depression. Peer rejection may also lead to dropping out of school, juvenile delinquency, or mental health problems.

Imagine you're having problems with another person. As adults, we know it can keep us distracted and make it difficult for us to concentrate on much else. Children are no different. Preschool education has been a major priority for educators and leaders across the country. One of the main goals of preschool education is to help children learn how to interact positively with each other. Children feel happier and are more adjusted to school when they have a friend. Parents and teachers must assist their children in making and being a friend so they can get the most out of their education.

This book is for parents and teachers who desire "polite" and "positive" children who have the needed interaction skills to form healthy relationships. Rejected children lack certain social rules of etiquette. This book breaks these rules down so you can develop and nurture them in your children. You are on the way to raising polite children who will form and keep the relationships necessary for success and avoiding bullying.

1

GOOD FRIEND?

Isabel, 9, comes home from school most days talking about how mean her best friend was to her. She says, "Francine didn't play with me today at recess; in fact, she made sure nobody played with me today. I hate recess and my best friend hates me." During the conversation, the phone rings—it's her best friend calling to chat. The next day the isolation recurs at recess. Does your child experience being "shut out" by his or her so-called friends on some occasions? Does your child have friends who are great when the kids are one-on-one and just plain mean in front of others? Is the topic of your child's school day consumed with negative issues regarding friends?

As a child grows and begins to walk, talk, and play, we constantly remind them to play nice, talk nice, and be nice. In fact, we usually reprimand them when they don't act nice toward others. In the park, we insist they share their toys with strangers. Unfortunately, parents and children get to know at a very young age that kindness and sharing is not always reciprocal. This can be, and is, frustrating for both parents and children.

Many days we encounter rude, disrespectful, and downright mean adults. It just takes one person with a poor attitude to put most people in a "bad mood" for a short while. Even though we should ignore these people, it just sometimes gets to us. We may even have to work or cooperate with a less than pleasant person.

For most children, the school day is no different. Personality, etiquette, and behavior are unique to every child and often cause friction and distress. As they grow up children must learn that friendship is a choice that determines their happiness and success. The choices our children make in friends play an integral role in how they develop and in the type of adults they will become. Children must be educated on what qualities make up a friend to enable them to make decisions on which students they decide to befriend. There are some questions that must be asked about those they choose as friends.

Here are some questions your children should ask themselves about their "friends":

- Do I have fun when I am with this friend?
- Do I feel good when I am with this person?
- Does he/she help me do well in school and activities?
- Does my friend treat me the same way when we are with other people?

I can still hear my parents saying time and time again, "You are known by the company you keep." If your children hang around ill-mannered children, you shouldn't be surprised when they imitate some of those less desirable behaviors. Children need other children, and the friends they make directly determine their attitudes and achievement in school.

Kids who hang around kids who do well in school also do well in school. Kids who view school and studying negatively are usually surrounded by kids with similar views. Parents should assist their children in choosing desirable qualities in friends and maintaining the relationships.

Make a list of qualities you and your child agree are essential to good friends. Discuss the qualities that are most important in friendships. Good friends are kind and welcoming. A friend will invite you to join in a game or discussion. Friends are people who make you smile and you enjoy being with.

Being kind and welcoming means being a person who is happy to see his or her friends and enjoys the company of those friends. Good friends don't have selective days when their friends are important and other days they aren't. Too often children come home upset that their "friend" was mean to them or wouldn't include them in a game or let them sit at their table during lunch. Parents must help children decide when it is time to terminate a friendship.

Some children are mean-spirited for different reasons. Children are often mean to others due to a lack of parenting or some type of dysfunction in the home. Parents and teachers who allow children to be "mean" by not correcting or discussing inappropriate behaviors foster children who are unkind to others. Other times, children are rude just to gain attention.

Educators should give attention to those children who consistently follow rules and treat others in a kind manner. As the parent, you must advise your child when to walk away from those who make them unhappy. Too often kids come home from school upset about their day, and the same child's name enters the conversation each time. A parent should repeatedly advise their child to end the relationship or remedy the situation. Teachers can and should discuss how friends and classmates should treat each other.

Around the age of eight, friends become very important to children. Children are never too young to start talking about the qualities they should look for in a friend. The number one quality is kindness. Children who are pleasant and thoughtful are good choices for friends. Kind people smile and point out nice things and take an interest in others. Parents and teachers should model this.

Friends share common interests. Have your child ask questions about other people's interests and find out who likes to do similar things. Some children are embarrassed to tell others of their interests for fear of being ridiculed. By encouraging your child to ask others about their interests your child will find out who participates in similar hobbies and activities and thus ease the fear of rejection or being made fun of.

Remind your child that just like a bag of apples, where there may be a spoiled fruit that is best put aside and not used in a pie, it is equally true with children in his or her class. Most likely, in your child's class there will be one or more children that your child should avoid. Teachers should watch these children carefully and contact their parents when mean or inappropriate behavior is exhibited. A child who is mean to anyone may display that nastiness toward your child as well. Explain the reality that it is unlikely for anyone to get along with everyone they meet and that they must know whom to avoid.

The guidelines are simple. Avoid kids who make you feel bad, but, if you do encounter someone who makes you feel bad, always act like a lady or gentleman. We should choose friends who are kind, inviting, and consistently nice. We need to teach our young ones to be nice to all, and if they experience poor treatment they should avoid those individuals.

Help your child feel confident about who he or she is. Other children easily detect this self-confidence. When your child looks in the mirror does he or she like the person he or she sees? Do you make it a regular habit to ask your child how he or she feels about him- or herself? As adults, when we feel confident about what we are wearing and feel good about ourselves, we have fun wherever we go. When we go out the door feeling poorly about our appearance or an outfit our outing is usually hindered because we are reserved and self-conscious. Do you compliment your child and help him or her to feel comfortable about his or her body and appearance? If your child is unhappy about a particular component of his or her physical appearance do you assist your child in making improvements or changing his or her self-image? We are not teaching them that appearance is everything and that what is inside doesn't count, but rather, we are being realistic and showing them that at their age appearance is important.

Children should dress comfortably and wear clothing to complement their body style. You have probably been walking in the mall and observed a person with clothes that were too tight, unflattering, or just plain ridiculous. Children should be shown how to dress for success by providing them with clothing that is flattering, appropriate, and "cool."

Two brothers, Andrew, 9, and Edward, 11, are best friends but completely different. The older brother is the super athlete and the younger brother is artistic and creative. Andrew, the little brother, is the last child picked for a soccer game at recess. In fact, Andrew would rather sit on the sidelines and watch, but the teacher makes everyone play. Andrew usually just tries his best to avoid the ball and concentrates on cheering for his team. Andrew lacks the interest, ability, and coordination to excel at most sports. Andrew likes to ride his bike and fish, but dropped out of organized sports at age seven when he realized that being the worst player wasn't cool any more. Edward, the older brother, plays most sports and frequently receives the "game ball" and cheers from the crowd. Although both are very different they both have an abundance of friends and a healthy sense of self.

The parents of Andrew and Edward have always made sure to praise their children's accomplishments and help them to feel good about their talents. They understand that for children to make friends they must feel good about themselves. Children must recognize what they do well, what they enjoy, and what they may or may not be best suited for.

You must know your child and help him or her develop talents and select interests that fit his or her capabilities. We wouldn't tell our children to pursue a career in singing if the sound of their voice made us cringe. If they enjoy singing it is best done for fun rather than for a career. Help your child recognize his or her abilities. Help your child to recognize that he or she is special and has a lot to contribute. Remind your child that no one is great at everything and that it is important to feel comfortable with what he or she can do well; those things your child does just okay he or she should probably seek help with or avoid. Parenting involves helping children recognize their strengths and weaknesses and feel comfortable and good about themselves.

When children feel confident about their strengths they are less likely to feel bad when others point out some area of weakness. Children and adults alike can benefit from being able to joke about something they may not excel in.

During physical education, a child who may not be the best athlete will feel better about not hitting the ball or making it to base when the child realizes that there are other things he or she does better. Help your child feel good about everything he or she does and reinforce the idea that we should always try to do our best. Make sure they understand that they don't have to be the best, but that they should always try their best. We should all learn to laugh about the things we may struggle with and enjoy our best attempts.

Every day must be treasured and enjoyed and we must help our children seek out people who make us happy. Children who smile are usually with other children who are smiling. Those kids who are negative, angry, and critical are usually surrounded by the same. The crowds they hang out with define your child's image.

When children start to worry too much about what their friends may say or how their friends think or react to things, it is time to question them about the reasons they are worrying. Remind them that friends are people you should be excited about sharing news and information with, not fearful of a reaction that may be degrading or humiliating. Friends are precious and special and choosing them should require serious thought and consideration.

When your child first meets a friend, he or she may not know if that person is going to be someone who will become a long lasting part of his or her life. Despite your child's best efforts the person may not be someone who brings companionship and joy. If this person is one who will be a positive companion, your child must know the important characteristics for being a good friend in return.

Children must learn that they will not always agree with their friends and that is okay. Children need to learn that they may have different views from their friends' views and that is okay. If they can't agree about a place to go or game to play there is an appropriate way to express themselves. Instead of refusing or making a sarcastic remark, your child might try saying, I would prefer to do this, maybe we can do your activity first and then mine.

Children and adults alike must learn to accept people the way that they are. If they meet someone, they must accept the fact that they won't agree with everything that person says or does. Being forceful or trying to change people is not the best way to make and keep a good friend.

Kids also need to learn that they don't have to always have an answer for everything on every subject. No one likes a person who always has an opinion about or knows everything. Sometimes it is nice just to be a listener and not comment about a topic. By being a good listener you show friends that they are interesting and you are happy to hear what they have to say. Constantly interrupting is rude and makes the other person feel they aren't important. This is good to remember about your own children. When they want to talk, you should do your best to stop everything and listen.

When meeting new people, tell your child "less is more." Help your child understand he or she doesn't need to share every little detail of his or her life. It is a good idea to share some positive and interesting things about his or her hobbies and likes. It is usually not a good idea to open up about personal and sensitive issues in the beginning. It is okay to talk about personal troubles now and then, but no one really wants to hear about negative things or "bad news" all the time.

One afternoon Amanda, 15, comes home crying that everyone was talking about her kissing this boy at school, even her closest friends. She even overheard her friends spreading the rumor.

Help your child be a good friend by avoiding petty cruelty and resisting the spreading of rumors. Teach your child the importance of trust among friends. If someone shares a secret, your child shouldn't talk about it with others unless the subject warrants telling an adult for intervention. Don't drag other people into disagreements. Friends should keep their issues private and settle disputes in a positive manner.

Remind children that friendships don't always work out but they should always be friendly with everyone. Friends are special and shouldn't be taken for granted. Help your children surround themselves with friends that make them smile. Children must stand tall as they meet new people. Tell them that nothing beats a smile; help them speak positively and listen when others talk.

FRIENDSHIP ACTIVITY
AND CONVERSATION STARTERS

Rank the order of importance for the following characteristics of a friend.
For older children:

- Has "cool" parents
- Does well in school
- Dresses well
- Is smart
- Brings a good school lunch
- Knows all the gossip
- Makes me laugh
- Doesn't pick on others
- Has good manners
- Is nice to me
- Invites me to join activities
- Shares my interests

For younger children:

- Shares toys
- Takes turns
- Never hits
- Has the same toy as me
- Listens to the teacher/their mommy

2

WE, NOT I

Ashley, 13, and Virginia, 14, have been friends and cheerleaders since they were seven years old. Ashley has been the captain for three consecutive years. When it comes time to try out for the high school squad, both girls are so excited and already making plans for their games. Virginia, like always, turns to Ashley for tips and practice to prepare for try-outs. To the surprise and shock of both girls, Virginia makes it and Ashley doesn't. Ashley's mother, although disappointed and hurt for her daughter, helps her to overcome the problem and feel motivated to keep practicing and try out again.

The response from Ashley's mother: Do you know how hard it is for a judge who doesn't know any of you girls dressed alike doing the same thing for just a few moments and have to make a choice of just a select few to be on a team? Admit you know they are sad and that you are sad to see them this way. Remind them there is something good in store for them, they just haven't found it yet. Have them call their friend and tell her that they are happy for her. It is fine to share that you are very disappointed but will definitely be at the first game to see her cheer. Even though making contact might be awkward, it is important to help your children release their tears and fears and move forward. Instill that avoidance is never really an answer and that you are able to rise above defeat and always support the team.

Marco, 9, is on a baseball team and practices and tries but often strikes out. His parents always tell him that all that matters is to try his best and that they are very proud of him. His teammates are not always so compassionate about his lack of skill. They often say things like, "We are losing because of you" and "We wish you weren't on our team."

The response from Marco's parents: Marco's parents are frustrated and feel bad for their son. They have spoken to some of the parents on the team and things have gotten a little bit better. Sometimes as a parent we do need to step in and help our child. We can't blame anyone, but by mentioning to the other parents the problem, their children stopped the behavior. To their son, they had to address that he must keep trying and learn to joke and laugh about his playing ability and keep practicing. It isn't the end of the world to struggle and if other kids realize that theur mean comments don't affect him, they will stop. Remind him that when he does get better, he shouldn't do this to the new or struggling player. A very important rule of etiquette is: be a good sport and team member. Parents should help children keep positive attitudes in all situations that teams encounter.

We are not born knowing how to work with others. Parents must teach their kids how to do this. The skills necessary to work effectively in teams are necessary throughout a person's life both in and out of the classroom. For marriage, jobs, sports, and friendships to be successful and pleasurable we must learn to work together and gain a true understanding of teamwork and respect.

It can't just be all about you. No one wants to listen to someone talk only about him- or herself all day long. Additionally, we grow tired of someone who is continually looking for attention or trying to be in the spotlight. Being part of a team and sharing glory and defeat together is a big part of childhood. Giving your best for the team is essential to getting along and participating with others.

What is your definition of teamwork? Does your definition include the kinds of behaviors and attitudes that go into effective teamwork? Do you model how to be a team player, get along with others, and work toward a common goal?

In the education of your child, you are working in a team consisting of you the parent, the teachers, and the administrators. Are you a good team member? Have you taken the time to get to know your child's teacher? Principal? Are you contributing to the team? Do you make regular contact with your child's teacher? Do you attend school events when possible? Are you familiar with the curriculum your child is learning? Do you understand the assessments and how any gaps in your child's education are being addressed? Do you really know how well your child is doing in school?

As a teacher, in the education of your student, you are working in a team consisting of you the teacher, the parents, and the administrators. Are you a good team member? Have you kept the parent informed to the best of your ability?

There is a connection between home and school that must be nurtured. Does your child understand his or her role as a team member to ensure success at school? Why do many parents experience difficulty with their children when it comes to school? Simply put, it is because children are often not carrying out their part of the bargain when it's time for school. Because of this, parents become frustrated and it hampers their relations with their child.

When children don't hold up their share of responsibility when it comes to friendships with other kids, the same result occurs: frustrated kids and a dampened relationship. Who would want to be paired with a person who consistently disregards the overall good of the group by not doing his or her share? You wouldn't put up with someone at work who consistently didn't give his or her best effort and didn't show consideration for the overall task and result.

So how do you teach kids to think "we" and not "I"? It's easier than you think. Explain to your kids that a team is a group of people who share a common objective and need to work together in order to achieve it. A band can't put on a concert without working together and everyone doing his or her part. We must teach our children they cannot achieve everything alone and must often use their talents and expertise in a team effort.

Working as a team is a great way to help kids make new friends. Teams offer opportunities for them to get to know someone else and for others to get to know them. Remind your child that being a good team member helps kids realize how nice and caring you are.

For children to be successful on a team, they must learn to compromise and trust others. They must also be someone who can be trusted. It is safe to say that no one wants to be around someone who is untrustworthy and who will be a consistent disappointment.

Not being picked for a team can be devastating for a child. Being the last one picked is often just as bad. Be sure there are no characteristics that your child is displaying which cause him or her to be last or not picked at all. Why are some children not chosen for a given team? It could be as simple as the child not knowing any of the other children. It is important for you to help your child make friends in class or in the activity he or she participates in. Get to know the other kids and their parents at least to the point your child is able to greet other children by their names and vice versa.

Sometimes, kids are so dominant that others don't want them on a team because they make all the decisions and stifle others' thoughts and desires. Be sure your child has a full understanding of other's opinions and when they should ask others before making final decisions. Being told what to do or bossed around once in a while is okay. When you are frequently "bossed" around, you eventually try to avoid being associated with that person.

Don't take for granted that your child is knowledgeable of other's feelings and desires. Parents must model consideration, thinking of others and group decision making in order to be fair and democratic in their dealings with others. This doesn't mean they can't ever be the decision-makers. It just means they can't be the controller all the time. Compromising is a skill that needs constant reminding and reinforcing.

As parents, we are used to compromising all the time. In our relationships and dealings with our children, we usually have to sacrifice some of our own feelings or needs from time to time. Even when we are exhausted, we still care for our children. We don't decide to not provide dinner because we are not hungry on a given night.

Discuss compromising and help your child realize that we all compromise everyday. Sometimes it is in our favor and we are ecstatic, and other times we might be a little less thrilled. We must learn to work together and respect other's opinions. You are probably wondering how to teach your kids this.

First, you must practice what you preach. When appropriate, discuss sacrifices you made for others. When it is your turn to have things your way share that too. Try saying, "Last week I let your aunt go out and I watched your cousins even though I wanted to go too. This weekend your aunt is going to babysit while I go to a movie I want to see."

You also may have a child, or come across a child, who always has great ideas but never carries them out. Explain how this is annoying to others and that just thinking up the idea isn't enough, you must also help to make it a reality. Brainstorm a list of traits your child has found annoying in others. Share the traits you find annoying as well. Honestly and kindly discuss any characteristics your child may tend to have or present at times.

The family is a great example of a team working together with a common goal of happiness and prosperity for all. We teach our children compromise as it is highly unlikely that every moment of every day will be pleasing and suiting to each member of the family. Younger siblings are often dragged to the events of older children. Play time is cut short because another child has homework or an event to go to.

Some days a particular member of the family is the leader and decision-maker and other times that person must step back and let another shine and have his or her moment. Children must be harmonious together. They must learn the reality of teams and how there are ups and downs and wins and losses and that is okay and normal. Being in a team means it is not always about you, but definitely involves you.

Think about evenings when your goal is to get everyone bathed, fed, and prepared for the next day with clean clothes and homework and studying done. This is a great example of teamwork where your child is an integral part of either success or failure. The way the child fares in the home has a direct impact on how he or she will fare in school and organized activities.

If you really think about it, being a parent of only one or several on a daily basis is like a strategic plan. Unlike organized sports, we don't get practices or have a game plan; in fact, often we rely on survival of the fittest. If we want our children to get along with others, we have to help them get along in the home.

After all, it isn't every day you are celebrating a great grade in school or a lost tooth, but rather general daily routines. Other times, it is dealing with someone who cheated, an illness, or a planned event that got rained out. We still must stay positive and work as a family to get through it all. If we as parents lose our cool in times of stress or change, be certain your children will follow in your footsteps both in and out of the home. "Wait your turn" and "We can't do that right now" become normal parts of life and not great disappointments or reasons to quit and fall apart.

ACTIVITY AND CONVERSATION STARTERS

Things to go over with your children:

- To Mom and Dad you are always number one, but when it comes to teams and groups of other children there are times for everyone to be number one.
- When it comes to competition, there is only a select group of winners. Sometimes there is just one and other times there are ten. You will have days you win and days you are left out. Remind your children of the saying, "If at first you don't succeed try and try again."
- Jealousy has no place in sports. One day you will have a friend who makes a team you don't. It is okay and normal to feel disappointed; however, you must ensure you are supportive and happy for that friend. You will one day be in the place where you are the one who made it and a true friend was left out; that person will need your support and comfort. What this really means is don't be nasty and degrading when you aren't a part of something and don't be smug and brag when you are.

HOME OR CLASSROOM ACTIVITY

Have the child list his or her strengths and weaknesses.

3

DO UNTO OTHERS

Henry, 10, comes home from school talking about his new best friend and how they had a great time at lunch. He says that he is now at the coolest lunch table. Henry says, "We all laughed and laughed, and I almost didn't get to finish my lunch." When asked what was so funny, he states, "We were laughing at this weird kid." When his mom looks puzzled, he says, "Don't worry mom, he knows he's weird and that we laugh at him."

KINDNESS TODAY?

Does your child always treat others kindly? Unfortunately, today's world tends to be filled with cruel and rude behavior that seems to be commonplace and almost acceptable. School bullying and domestic violence make the news way too often. Parents must make a conscious effort to help their children be kind, gentle, and sensitive to the feelings and needs of others. Ridiculing others just to fit in is just as wrong as doing it directly.

You are not alone in looking for ways to battle the continual exposure to violence that may leave kids desensitized to "mean" behavior. We must foster feelings that allow our children to put themselves "in someone else's shoes." Your children must know the difference between right and wrong in every aspect of behavior.

DEVELOPING COMPASSION

Mary, 7, watches her brother play video games where everyone's object is to kill as many invaders as possible. The more people getting killed, the more points you score. Should we be surprised when she doesn't understand that when she threw a rock at recess and hit someone unintentionally she should apologize? She must be reprimanded, first, for throwing a rock and second, for hitting an unsuspecting person. One thoughtless action leads to another.

Parents play an integral role in encouraging their children to become caring individuals with a well-developed sense of empathy. Children must be nurtured to bring out a caring response to those in need. Modeling kindness and reminding children to respond to friends, classmates, and all those who are hurting is the first step to raising kind children. Just as we should correct our children when they display behavior that is mean or uncaring, we must praise acts of kindness and compassion. We are the role model and how we act and what we say set the example.

Some children need direction in identifying which behaviors are kind and which are cruel. When you show that kind behavior is a priority, your children will follow your lead. Take the time to discuss emotions that may show that a certain behavior or comment may have been hurtful. If siblings are fighting and one ends up in tears, discuss the action that led to the pain and suffering of the other.

Explain that people cry when they are hurt, mentally as well as physically. Hurting doesn't have to come from something physical, like an injury or illness. Hurting can come from unkind words, actions, and jokes. Again, emphasize to your child that if he or she joins in these actions it is the same as if he or she initiated them. Teachers should discuss complicity. A student that is present in the commission of an inappropriate act of another student constitutes condoning of the incident. Simply stated, they are just as wrong to stand and watch or join in these behaviors.

TEACHING ACCEPTABLE BEHAVIOR

Kevin, 9, and Mari, 7, are in constant battle in the back seat of the car. Kevin teases his sister and picks on her until it results in pushing and shoving. Mom and Dad are constantly asking them to stop. The peace lasts for only minutes before returning. Mom threatens to leave one of them home next time but never carries out the threat.

Do your children fully understand your expectations for their behavior everywhere and every time? If your warnings regarding unacceptable behavior are ignored, take appropriate action to get respect. You can enforce proper behavior without displaying inappropriate behavior. With love and kindness you can still enforce the rules.

Let your kids know exactly what kind of behavior you do and don't like. Model being caring and kind to others. Be sure your actions toward your own children model and teach kindness as well. Parents who are consistent and compassionate raise children who are consistent and compassionate. Most parents have experienced moments when they are less than pleased with their child. It is very easy to lose control and "go crazy." Even when we feel like yelling, screaming, or insulting, we must stop and rethink our actions. Children who are continually belittled learn to belittle others. Believe me, as the mother of two boys, I have felt pushed over the limit, but I try to take a deep breath and count to ten before lashing out when my children do something wrong.

Kids need to learn that they may feel frustrated, disappointed, and hurt but should always respond politely and respectfully. You may be wondering how to do that; the secret is to practice what you preach. Discipline and correct your children firmly, clearly, and compassionately. The goal for disciplining children should be to reduce or eliminate the undesirable behavior, not to make the child feel guilt or "bad."

In other words, respond the way you would want your child to if they were correcting another. Remember, "Do as I say, not as I do" sends the wrong message to kids. You must model and preach the golden rule, "Treat others as you would like to be treated." Also make sure that caregivers and those who spend a lot of time with your children model and teach as you do.

PRACTICE WHAT YOU PREACH

Barbara talks to her two children about behaving and speaking nicely. In fact, she has purchased an entire book series on manners. However, too often when her children step out of line, she raises her voice and uses words she wouldn't want them to repeat. Barbara is not setting the right example. Children look to their parents for direction on how to behave and actions speak louder than words. When we don't speak harshly we feel better and later have no regrets and no need to apologize.

Parents are extremely busy and often have difficulty getting through their workweek, household chores, and obligations. You may not have time to model kindness through volunteer work and charity, but most people can certainly find nice things to do for family members in and outside the home. Children who are treated with dignity, kindness, and love are more secure. Kindness and respect encourage repeat behavior.

Here are some ideas to model the golden rule for both parents and children:

- Read to a sibling.
- Help a neighbor in his or her yard.
- Write a letter to a grandparent or relative who lives far away.
- Stand up for someone who is teased at school.
- Pray for someone who is sick.
- Collect for a charity.
- Donate small clothing or old toys to the poor.
- Praise someone for a job well done.
- Show movies and read books that send messages of compassion and kindness.
- Monitor television programs that may send messages you don't want your kids to view.

FOSTERING SELF-ESTEEM

In helping your children to grow socially and "fit in" at school you must evaluate and concentrate on their self-esteem. Kids need to feel good about themselves in order to get along with others. Living the golden rule of treating others as you want to be treated starts with feeling good about yourself.

Remember, self-esteem and self-respect go hand in hand. Children learn to love and respect themselves by having others love and respect them. Even when under stress and extreme frustration, you should never put down your child. This will help your child to understand how to treat others. Your children will model your behavior, both the desirable and the undesirable.

Your goal is to help them make friends who will help them make positive choices so they will ultimately live happy lives. No one likes a person who is sarcastic, degrading, or disrespectful. Don't provide any poor examples for them to follow. Help them feel good about themselves by listening to their concerns. Express worries you had as a child. By expressing yourself you will help your child relate to you, and in turn allow yourself to be an integral part of your child's life when he or she needs you most.

Children need to be taught to respect themselves and to refuse to endure and accept disrespect. Respect and discipline go hand in hand. Parents will always have to discipline their children, but how you do it will determine your child's respect for you as well as for others.

When a child does not listen or respond to a request we can model mutual respect by delaying a privilege or pleasurable activity. Speak to your child in tones you would like to hear from him or her and listen when your child speaks to you. Avoid criticizing in order to teach your child about earning respect. Minimize your child's mistakes and focus on what he or she does right. Express appreciation for positive behavior. Acknowledge your child's progress and avoid demanding perfection, your goal is to develop a well-rounded, educated lady or gentleman. And most of all, listen to your child's dreams and aspirations, excite your child about his or her life and future, and make your child want to be all that he or she can be.

CURRENT REALITY

Playgrounds should not resemble jungles where predator-prey relationships help maintain a balance. Schools should not be an example of survival of the fittest. Everyone deserves equal respect and all children should be kind and play together harmoniously.

Ideally, this is true, but realistically, we know this is not the case. There are different cliques and groups with both "cruel" and kind children. Kids are often worried about the unstructured part of the school day, times like lunch and recess. They never know if they are going to have fun or be the object of the fun. Some join in cruel behavior just to be part of the clique. By teaching children to treat others as they want to be treated we can help them to pick a side and practice what they have learned at home.

No child enjoys being ridiculed, left out, or teased. Are you wondering if your child can separate right from wrong and cruelness from kindness? Be sure that by educating and influencing them properly in your own home children can "fight back" and still foster kindness and compassion and eliminate bullying.

CRUEL KIDS OR BULLIES?

Michael, 8, loves school and especially recess after lunch. He plays with a group of boys and draws pictures of dragons and other magical figures. Michael never plays sports during recess like the majority of the boys. Drawing is his joy, and playing soccer or catch isn't his idea of fun. His mother almost faints when he comes home asking what "fag" and "gay" mean. Do Michael's parents realize that he is a victim of bullying? Do they know how to help him?

Mary, 11, hasn't reached puberty yet. She was raised on a small farm and is an avid horseback rider. In elementary school, she would wear jeans and horse t-shirts to school and enjoyed recess, lunch, and all the fun activities at school, and was an exceptional student. In middle school, she is called a boy and tortured by many girls in her class. They tell everyone that her boyfriend is a horse. They constantly touch the back of her shirt and announce to the class that she doesn't wear a bra. The truth is that until she enters ninth grade she doesn't need one. She spends the majority of her middle school years just hiding from the group of "mean girls" to avoid further embarrassment. Her mother consistently reminds her that she is a great student and these girls are just jealous that she has such a neat hobby and is nice. She has many "sad" afternoons, but somehow her mom has the magic words to help her cope. She tells her, "Just laugh with them when they say mean things and act like it doesn't bother you." Fortunately, this time passes quickly, and high school is much more pleasurable.

In my experiences, as a teacher and administrator in public and private schools, and additionally as a professor talking with school administrators across the country, I have had firsthand experience with almost every type of bullying situation. I have seen very kind children be teased and bullied, and when handled properly by parents, teachers, and schools, the children usually rise above it.

As a mom, I have had my own children come home upset by "comments" or "problems" with friends. I began taking note of the characteristics shared by both bullies and victims. In sharing these, I hope to assist parents in helping their children to avoid bullying and reach their potential in school. For many years, I continually thought about all the "tricks" that help children achieve and realized that many of them were easy to carry out, but far too often not utilized.

Over the years I have engaged in conferences with parents both over the phone and in person. These conferences shed light on how specific parenting skills and discussions can and have significantly reduced, prevented, and eliminated incidents of bullying. It was then that I knew parents needed to realize that they can make a difference. It is as easy as recognizing and understanding bullying and taking the proper measures to end it.

There are warning signs everywhere in our lives: directions, traffic, medicines, and food preparation to name a few. Unfortunately, when it comes to bullying and cruel teasing in school, there are often no obvious signs until emotional scars surface. In today's halls of learning and during the unstructured part of the school day, bullying and teasing affect far too many children. Parents must, and should, be aware of what to look for and how to help their children defend themselves.

Unfortunately, we only talk about it until it leads to violent and unbelievable behavior that makes headlines. What makes a child withdraw, become anorexic, or lose faith or belief in him- or herself and his or her capabilities? There is a hidden epidemic spreading through our schools and its name is bullying. Children, parents, and teachers are seeking information and assistance for this hurtful epidemic. Why do some children rise above it? Why are others pulled down into depression, despair, and isolation? Why isn't it discussed and why aren't children given the power to escape it? Why do children prefer to suffer in silence rather than share their experiences and concerns with their parents or teachers?

The only way to stop this harmful behavior is to recognize it, discuss it, confront it, and solve it. The following pages will inform and empower you to help your child avoid bullying and enjoy school days in and out of the classroom.

ACTIVITY AND CONVERSATION STARTERS

Parent/Teacher Reflection Activity

To determine where you are in modeling the golden rule of treating others as you would like to be treated, ask yourself these questions:

- Do I speak to my child/student as I would like to be spoken to?

- Do conversations of compassion and kindness enter family discussions/classrooms?
- Does my child exhibit behaviors he or she wouldn't appreciate in others?
- Does my child act one way when I'm present and differently when I'm absent? (Find out!)
- How well do I really know my child's friends?
- Do I really spend enough time understanding the social needs of my child/student?
- Do I follow through on my obligations of proper role modeling?

CONVERSATION STARTER

Sit down with your child or in small groups of children and ask them names they have been called that they hope won't be repeated.

4

BE AWARE OF BULLIES!

Another important rule for parents is: be knowledgeable. Parents need to know what bullying is and recognize it when it occurs!

Homework, tests, and racing around are hard enough without the dreaded words "I hate school," and "I have no friends." Even worse, sometimes our children seem withdrawn, fragile, and depressed and we can't figure out what is wrong.

As a mother, teacher, and school administrator, I am here to tell you that you are not alone. Parents' concern over their child's social well-being and fear that their child may be bullied is far too common. However, the fact remains, parents can prevent and stop bullying and teasing that is directed at their child.

Unfortunately, even in preschool, kids come home sad about comments or "bad moments" with classmates. Today, school has become more than a place of learning; it is also a place of socialization where certain cruel incidents and words can leave scars on a child's self-esteem. School success is not just about the ABCs today. When we wish for our child to be successful in school, we often are thinking about his or her social life, as well as academics.

When your child comes home from school crying, it may be frustrating and even devastating for you, as well as for him or her. We as parents strive to give our children every opportunity to live a happy and fulfilling life. I want to help you be sure that you are educated in helping your child "fit in" at school and enjoy all aspects of his or her education. By reading these pages, the "how and whys" bullying occurs, and how to avoid the negative effects of bullying and teasing, you will better understand bullying and how to protect your children from it.

Too often, children tease and taunt each other. Parents often feel helpless and don't know where to begin to help their child feel good and respond to these situations. Even worse, sometimes parents are unaware that their child is being verbally attacked until it ends in undesirable consequences such as poor grades or inappropriate behavior.

You, as parents, must be informed about the signs of bullying and the ways to deal with it. Whether you have had a child who has been or is being bullied, or just are seeking knowledge about bullying, know that you are not alone. Rest assured that incidents of teasing and bullying can be reduced and even eliminated. However, you must realize there are many shapes and forms of bullying. By the end of this chapter you should feel confident in recognizing bullying beyond the black eye.

Teachers must be the eyes and ears for parents. Bullying occurs in our schools and teachers can help inform parents and school administrators of situations that occur.

Does your child experience these types of scenarios regarding teasing and bullying?

Tatiana, 13, spends at least several days a week in tears over being excluded from her regular group of friends at school. She often worries about going to school and being ignored by her peers. The stares, glares, and giggles behind her back have made her lose confidence and have taken the enjoyment out of the school day and instilled anxiety on a daily basis.

Christopher, 7, is always praised by his teachers, parents, and relatives for his adorable big cheeks. In school, his peers remind him regularly that his tummy is also big. He often comes home and asks his mother if he is fat.

Sally, 9, got her first pair of eyeglasses over the summer before fourth grade. They were pink, and she was so excited to wear them on the first day of school. The excitement died down when a few students called her names, such as four eyes, and told her she looked like a bug with her glasses on. One day a little boy removed them from her desk and stepped on them.

Kelly, 6, bought new sneakers for school with purple butterflies and glitter—she thought they were the greatest. A group of girls in her class decided that anyone with butterflies on their shoes could not be in their play group at recess. The next day she didn't wear the shoes and still was not permitted in the play group. The new reason was that anyone with pigtails was not allowed. In fact, every day there seemed to be a reason to exclude her.

Kara, 12, wears a belt to school every day and pulls it so tight to make her look thinner that it leaves a mark. She refuses to eat lunch at school and comes home with a headache most days. She constantly cries in her room and tells her mother she hates school.

Raising children today may often be an exhausting task. It involves a lot more than loving, nourishing, and educating your children to be their own person. Understanding the world around us and the sometimes harsh reality and cruelty exhibited by some is a must in helping children develop. Preparing children for their future means helping them grow intellectually, socially, mentally, and physically. Time spent in school impacts a great deal of your child's waking hours and determines a great deal of his or her personality, confidence, and effort.

A lot of attention is given to serious incidents of violence and weapons in school, which, thankfully, most children do not face on a daily basis. However, many children do face bullies and teasing on a regular basis. According to the U.S. Justice Department, one in four children is bullied every day. When we send a child to school, we are not always sure they are able to reach their potential. It is a parent's responsibility to know why and take action. Too often, teasing, taunting, exclusion, and hitting, often termed bullying, are a part of a student's day in one form or another.

School bullying is a nationwide problem that many students find difficult to escape. Children exposed to this ridicule often suffer from absences, poor grades, violent behavior, and low self-esteem. Bullies and their victims need the support, understanding, and guidance of parents, schools, and the community. Nobody has the right to hurt another person. School should be a place of discovery and learning not torment and anguish.

You may recall the many times you have asked yourself if the tears and complaints are just a part of normal childhood games or something to be concerned with. Parents must be in tune with what happens in their child's unstructured part of the school day and have the knowledge of how to distinguish the "normal kid stuff" from the "harmful kid stuff." Too often bullying goes undetected by parents and schools. Additionally, it is rarely discussed and often absent from school rules and policies. Sometimes, when addressed, it is handled ineffectively and both the bullies and victims are left feeling lost with no solutions for prevention, which causes them to withdraw and not discuss the issues.

Bullying is a pattern of behavior where one child uses physical or mental tactics to belittle another, usually chosen for his or her vulnerability. The abuse is abrasive and if left unchecked will wear down a child's self-image. Research has suggested that many students are and will continue to be bullied unless some form of action is taken. Generally, bullying tends to continually increase through elementary school, peak in the middle school years, and taper off in high school, explaining why younger children are so vulnerable. Sometimes bullying is viewed as harmless and a normal part of growing up. However, it is not a part of normal childhood conflict and should never be dismissed as such. Teasing and taunting is bullying when it is not reciprocal. This means that bullying occurs when it lowers another's self-esteem and is one-sided. The joke is constantly on one student. When two kids go back and forth at each other and laugh, that is not bullying. When one child never gives any of the same "nonsense" back to the other child, parents must recognize that the actions are most likely inappropriate.

We have all heard the saying "boys will be boys" and sometimes that is true. If two kids constantly compete and tease each other about who is faster or smarter, feelings might get hurt sometimes and that is okay. Johnny might say, "You stink" and Nick says, "Not as bad as you"—this is typical horseplay and silliness. It is easier than you think to find out whether your child's classmates are "friends" or bullies.

You must ask about all aspects of the school day, especially lunch, recess, and after school. Get the names of kids that are constantly mentioned, and keep track of the child whose name is always mentioned with fear, anger, or frustration. On the same note, keep track of the names that are usually associated with fun stories and smiles. Bullying and teasing are often done in a sneaky form that is hidden from the eye. Children must be prodded to discuss their school day and social interactions so parents are informed prior to any negative effects.

It is not enough to send your child to school and say, "Just focus on learning and do your work. I don't send you to school to socialize." People are social creatures and we send children to school to learn and to grow up to be successful contributing members of society. In actuality, the social aspect of school is critical. Your child's social skills are critical to his or her success in school and life.

We've all encountered people who are brilliant but were completely lacking in social skills. This type of person is difficult to deal with and often avoided regardless of the knowledge they possess. Teaching kids to interact with others and feel confident in who they are is critical to bully proofing your child and helping him or her to avoid kids who display cruel and unacceptable behavior.

As children grow, they start to see themselves by how their peers view them. We can tell our children how special they are and that we love them one hundred times a day, but there comes a point in each child's life when they need to hear it from others, especially their peers.

The problem with bullying is that it entails so many forms. We know it exists and it hurts our kids. Finding it and stopping it is not always easy, but it can be done. Years ago, kids would come home with a black eye and it was easy to tell they'd had a run-in with a schoolyard bully. Bullying is not just getting beaten up or having someone take your lunch or lunch money; it is sometimes done so discreetly that many children realize they're hurting but don't understand why and sometimes blame themselves.

Kids are cruel and sometimes our children need to let things go in one ear and out the other. Nevertheless, there is a line between what is not very nice behavior and what is bullying and unacceptable. Sometimes contact is not made and words are not even spoken, yet bullying is occurring. When a child is left out or continually stared at or glared at, bullying is occurring. Recognizing bullying means knowing what happens to your child during the school day and guiding him or her in a response. Ask questions, get your child to open up, and discuss what's bothering him or her and help your child to change and stop the bullying.

Sometimes you might be hesitant to ask direct questions to find out what is happening in school. There are questions to open the lines of communication without straight out asking if your child is being bothered or bullied. The response to these questions can help you determine the nature and seriousness of the problem. Some examples are:

- Would you like to invite some friends over tomorrow?
- What's happening in school?
- Are there any activities you want to join?
- Would you like to invite your best friend over for dinner?
- I remember when kids were picked on in school—it even happened to me. Does that happen in your school?
- Is there a kid in school who bosses everyone around and is even mean?
- Does anyone get picked on at school?
- Who did you sit with at lunch today?

John went to middle school and worried about changing classes, having six teachers, and taking final exams. John was a big kid, good looking, and smart too. He was shocked to find out the hardest part about middle school was the five minutes between each class and the thirty minutes for lunch, not to mention the dreaded physical education class and the boys' locker room. His clothes were hidden, his shoes stolen, and undressing in front of others made him stressed and nervous every day. One day, when he was standing on the basketball court two older kids pulled down his shorts and left him standing there in his underwear. John's mom and dad were devastated when he came home humiliated and ashamed over the day's events.

John's parents immediately took action. The physical education teacher was called and a conference was scheduled. They discovered that a certain group of boys in the eighth grade were bullying the younger students. The teacher was made aware of the incident with John, and the students involved were punished by the school. His parents prepped him for the next day by making him understand that he was the target of a nasty prank and he needed to be alert and stand up for himself. He was then able to face the other students and be on guard to prevent further "attacks."

What if John hadn't come home and talked about his problems with his parents? What if it had escalated into John retaliating and suffering disciplinary consequences from school? What if it had just continued and John's self-esteem dropped and his desire to do well in school dwindled? We as parents must help our children to survive the negative social aspects of school, as well as the positive ones. Thus, we provide them the opportunities for learning in a healthy atmosphere where they can grow and feel good about themselves.

FRIENDS CAN BULLY TOO!

It's important to mention that bullying can sometimes occur from within the child's circle of friends. This can often be more hurtful than being bullied by the "class bully" whom everyone knows and dislikes.

Christina, 11, and Laura are best friends. They tell each other everything, from the boys they like to fights with their siblings and struggles with their parents. Christina is shocked when other kids at school tease her about information only Laura knows. One friend says, "Is it true you like Rick? That's gross, he's a nerd!" Another says, "Your brother picks his nose and wipes boogers all over your stuff. I'm never borrowing something from you again." Christina comes home sad, angry, and crying on a regular basis. Christina's parents need to help her define what a true friend is. They help her understand that friends may come and go, and a person is lucky to hold on to a few dear ones. Their advice is that it takes time to choose a real friend and through interaction over time she would get to know who really is a true or sincere friend.

Chris, 8, has been getting warts since he was four. His mom puts medicine on his warts to get rid of them, and he has even gone to the dermatologist to get them burned off. Everybody in class starts laughing when someone has to sit next to Chris. His best friend, Joey, shouts, "Gross! You are going to get warts too. Don't touch me!" Later, he says he is sorry but does the same thing a few days later. Chris must tell his friend privately that his comments are hurting his feelings and ask him to stop. If Joey continues with the rude comments, Chris should find a new buddy to spend his time with. Chris knows that true friends stand by you and don't bring attention to your flaws.

Parents need to recognize that friends sometimes pick and choose ways to ridicule, tease, and isolate others. Once in a while, this may be hurtful, but tolerable. When a particular child keeps causing tears and anguish, that is the time to reevaluate the friendship. You may have to teach your child the old saying, "With friends like this, who needs enemies."

Even if your child is not being bullied right now, you must take action to ensure they don't become a target in the future. Remember, students are usually reluctant to tell anyone if they have been bullied. Most students who are bullied are often close to their parents, but many times they do not discuss bullying due to fear of retaliation by the perpetrator or fear of being labeled a tattle-tale. Many students have suggested that they do not feel adults can really help and thus don't talk about it. They also fear they may be viewed as weak or cowardly and need "mommy" to fight their battles.

As children grow, their dependence on peers for their image and sense of self-worth increases. Being bullied may lead to increased social isolation at school, as children will stay away from the victim for fear of being bullied themselves for the association. The bullied child feels unsupported and his or her image declines with each occurrence. Don't let this be an option for your child.

The first step in preparing children for the social part of school is to help them recognize the bully when they are confronted. If you aren't sure, then start investigating your child's friends, talk to the teacher or school administrator; keep asking until you get enough information to determine if your intervention is necessary.

Bullying is not equivalent to your child having occasional trouble with math or schoolwork. Bullying and teasing must be stopped immediately. You don't have a few months to see if things improve as you would with academic work. The consequences and negative results are too costly. You have to get involved and take action with any suspicion. Inquiring about the unstructured and social part of the day is a must.

Be sure to ask if there is a policy regarding bullying at your child's school. If you suspect your child has been bullied, ask the five essential questions: who, what, where, when, and how. Ask your child if any "friends" just stood by and watched. Find out if an adult was nearby.

Many kids who bully others have problems in their own home. They may have parents who lash out and punish harshly and inconsistently. You can't just tell your child to stand up and fight back, or tell them that the bully is often not aware his or her behavior is unacceptable and hurtful. However, when regular teasing occurs where there is a balance of power among children sometimes standing up and fighting back can help. When it comes to bullying, on the other hand, kids may need adult intervention. Many kids have tried to walk away or fight back but usually feel like it is their fault. Children often have a skewed picture of what has happened as a result of bullying. We, as parents, must help them see they are victims and the bully has the problem in need of assistance.

Hopefully you feel knowledgeable and prepared to help your child recognize when they are being bullied, and that together, you, the teacher, and the school can and will put an end to this inappropriate behavior.

ACTIVITY AND CONVERSATION STARTERS

Bullying Activity

Ask the child to describe behaviors that they would consider bullying.

Tips for Parents

- Talk to your children about their school day including lunch and recess.
- Discuss what bullying is and cases that have been on the news when age appropriate.
- Discuss what constitutes a friend.
- Maintain open communication that is understanding and nonjudgmental.
- Review the policy for bullying in your school with your child.

For the Teacher-Parent Relationship

Teachers and parents must communicate. Teachers see a side of children a parent may not. At school, your child may act very different from what you might expect. Parents and teachers need to communicate and devise an action plan to help children succeed. These discussions should focus on social as well as academic issues. Educators should orient parents to their way of thinking, to share their knowledge, and to teach parents how to support their children.

In the next chapter, reasons why certain children are targeted will be discussed.

5

BULLY BEWARE!

Why does bullying occur and why are certain children targeted? How can we reduce or eliminate negative situations? Sometimes bullying is viewed as harmless and a normal part of growing up. However, it is not a part of normal childhood conflict and should never be dismissed as such. Teasing and taunting is bullying when it is not reciprocal. This means that bullying occurs when it lowers another's self-esteem and is one-sided. An important rule for parents to follow is to be proactive to eliminate bullying.

Why does bullying occur and why are certain children targeted? Children may be victimized due to their physical appearance, such as weight or build. Other children who are quiet, passive, or just stand out for some reason, even a positive one, may be taunted as well. Sometimes children are bullies because they experience poor self-image and only feel good about themselves when putting down others. Both boys and girls involve themselves in the unfair treatment of others. Girls often tend to be hurtful and band together to isolate certain students.

Name-calling that makes a child anxious, angry, or unworthy will diminish a student's drive for education. Many times this will happen in front of their peers. Teasing can have severe and even lifelong consequences. Exposed to this type of abuse for a long time, these children will become incapable of reaching their potential. Bullying is a roadblock to learning which can and should be addressed so all students have the best opportunity for success.

Parents should watch for signs that indicate their child may be bullied and provide the support and guidance needed to break the destructive pattern. Children who are experiencing bullying may have certain obvious signs such as trouble sleeping, wanting to stay home from school excessively, and having few friends. Other signs may be bruising, torn clothes, and nervousness. In other cases, a child might be withdrawn and quiet, avoiding most social interaction.

As children grow, their dependence on peers for their image and sense of self-worth increases. Being bullied may lead to increased social isolation at school, as children will stay away from the victim for fear of being bullied themselves because of their association. Bullied children feel unsupported and their image declines with each occurrence.

Follow your instinct when you suspect your child is being bullied in school. Be honest and talk openly with your child about your concerns. If you find out your child may be suffering at the hands of others at school, don't panic and overreact. Instead take an active part to empower your child to deal with bullies, reduce victimization, and rebuild positive feelings. Bullies and their victims need our help.

A discussion of bullying with your child is the first step to intervention for reducing incidents. Share your own experiences if appropriate. Talk about ways your child could try to stop the perpetrators. Practice scenarios your child has experienced, going over exactly how your child should handle them and when to seek an adult. When necessary, notify the school and allow them to assist in remedying the situation. Never ignore the situation thinking it will pass by itself.

Parents must remind kids to move away from and rise above the kids who bother, insult, tease, and humiliate them. This can be done without resorting to unkind behavior. If inappropriate behavior persists, they must report it to an adult. If they don't feel comfortable telling someone at school then they should tell you. Help your child feel confident in standing up to "cruel kids."

Children who are cruel are usually trying to be popular or "cool." Others crave attention. Sometimes they don't realize they are really hurting someone else. When a child stands up to the person and stops paying attention, the behavior usually stops. It is important to spend time teaching your child how to deal with rude children. If your child has experienced tears at the hands of another child you must help them stick up for themselves. Continual poor treatment can have harmful long-term effects.

Teach your child to speak up and say "stop" and walk away. Help them make friends that are kind and above this type of action. Children may be victimized in many areas of the school day, in after-school activities, and on social occasions. You can't be everywhere, however you can know what's going on and how to protect them.

Whatever the reason bullying occurs, it must be addressed. Some kids bully others to prevent someone else from bullying them. Other times it is just to be "cool" or to get the attention of the "popular" kids. Others may exhibit this kind of behavior to feel good about themselves and feel they have control over something. The message must be sent to all kids that bullying, for any reason, is wrong and will not be tolerated.

So now you must be wondering how you can keep your child from being bullied or becoming a bully. This is something that you must work on every day. Open your eyes to the signals that should trigger your concern and assistance. Don't let the odds rule your child. Beat the odds by not being blinded and dismissing anything as kid stuff. Be the detective and be certain your child is safe and most of all happy most of the time. Although no police work is required of parents, raising kids today means being aware and letting your child know you are aware and will find out everything.

Watch your children in different situations. How do they react on a sports team, at a party, or playing in the park? Do they always let others make the decisions? Are they too aggressive? Are they too passive? Are their friends as in tune and concerned about the same things you are?

How do your children get along with their siblings and their siblings' friends? How do they treat other family members? Be on top of their behavior, always teaching and modeling how to treat others and how they should be treated.

Andre, 8, joins the baseball team and has never played before. In the beginning, he has a little trouble making contact with the ball. One day the coach divides the team in two to have a practice game. One player yells out how mad he is to have Andre on his team and that they would surely lose. This was voiced loud enough for the parents, coaches, and anyone watching the game to hear. Andre's mother does nothing. Shame on Andre's mother. No wonder this type of treatment is mimicked by other players later in the season. Don't let your child be rude or bully others. Teach your child to stand up to those who put them down. Andre's mother should have made him approach this child and say, "I am just starting, and soon you will be sorry for that comment." When other children see that they can tease others without reprimand, especially in a crowd, it is more likely they think it is okay and will continue.

Never discuss threatening to step in to diffuse the situation before using the proper channels. If a child is exhibiting bullying behaviors, they can be taught more appropriate ways of dealing with others. The process will take time, so be patient.

ACTIVITY AND CONVERSATION STARTERS

For the child being bullied:

- Show your child how to stay calm and not react to the bully. Sometimes when the bully does not get a reaction he or she will stop the teasing.
- Teach your child to be assertive and answer with a comeback or just agree.
  - For example: I do have glasses, thanks for noticing.
  - I could care less about what you say.
  - You are not the boss of me!
  - Keep your comments to yourself; I am not interested.
- Provide a warm and positive environment in your home. Provide an atmosphere where you can ask questions.

CONVERSATION STARTERS

- Does anyone get teased in your class?
- Has anyone ever picked on you in school?
- You know that you can talk to me about anything, right?
- I remember how tough school relationships can be.

Open the lines of communication. Share with your child any experiences you have had or witnessed with bullying and teasing, such as:

- I remember when I was teased in third grade for my new glasses . . .

- Children used to hurt my feelings, I remember when a boy in my class continually embarrassed me about . . .
- Recognize that bullying is never acceptable and should not be overlooked.
- Be an advocate for an antibullying policy in your child's school if you do not have one already.
- Discuss complicity and talk about what should be done if your child witnesses bullying behaviors. Encourage your child not to be a passive bystander but to seek assistance from an adult.
- Talk with the school and the parents of the bully to formulate a plan to stop the behavior and include the children in the planning.

For the Child Who Is the Bully

- Try to avoid physical or harsh discipline. Children exposed to hostile behavior usually have poor problem-solving skills.
- Be consistent with discipline.
- Teach your child empathy for others. Share how you feel when your child exhibits bullying behaviors.
- Provide some opportunities for you and your child to do some community service. This gives your child a chance to experience attention for kind and compassionate behavior.
- Unfortunately, the world often shares negative behaviors more than the positive. Allow your child the opportunity to witness others being kind.
- When you feel you are unable to help your child change his or her behavior, seek the help of a child psychologist.

Remember, children are often reluctant to share that they are being teased. Know that every child will experience a few unhappy days. Parents must look for signs and cues that their child is being bullied. When "bad" days seem to be the majority and behaviors and attitudes change, you must be prepared to help your child open up and confront the bully. Teachers must keep parents informed of any signs and cues that they need to watch or address. Reassure them that telling on others is sometimes difficult, but necessary.

6

HALF FULL
OR HALF EMPTY?

Stephanie, 14, gets so excited about picking out her outfits for her classmates' weekly birthday parties. Many of her Hispanic friends are turning fifteen and having huge celebrations where she even gets the opportunity to put on long dresses and gowns. When she goes shopping with her mom, they sometimes spend hours and hours picking out the right dress. She is thrilled to wear this dress until her good friend Lauren comes over and makes weird faces and little innuendos that the dress is not very pretty and certainly not flattering. Every time Stephanie goes out with Lauren, she feels self-conscious and spends most of the time worrying about her appearance instead of the event. Lauren's comments are subtle but strong enough to make Stephanie doubt her appearance and lose confidence. As a result, Stephanie can't enjoy herself at the event.

Stephanie's parents are frustrated because no matter what they buy to help Stephanie feel good, the same friend continually brings her down, but Stephanie continually begs to invite her over, with the same result. Stephanie's parents need to bring up the topic of Lauren and ask their daughter if she is sure that Lauren is the type of friend she wants, and if she ever has a good time with this girl. Stephanie's parents need to guide her in seeking new friends and to help her make better choices.

As parents, we have to teach our children right from wrong. Today, right from wrong is much more than simple yes or no decisions and goes beyond staying in school and not doing drugs. Right from wrong involves personal decisions that define your children and allow them to grow into happy and successful adults. We must help our children to know when they are being oversensitive or making the wrong choice.

Sometimes children look for the negative part of the school day rather than rejoice in the good things. Negative children grow into negative adults, and we certainly want to prevent this. When your child comes home talking about how someone did something to them or that someone didn't speak to him or her today, try to change the subject to get your child to tell you about something positive that occurred. Teach them to dwell on the positive.

Nearly everything our children worry about and focus on is determined by what the adults in their lives are worrying about and focusing on. My nieces will come home wanting to talk about the dirty looks they received at school and the snide remarks they heard from their fellow students. It is not always easy, but my sister and I redirect the conversation to the good things that happened to them.

The old saying "misery loves company" must not be applied to our family life. We, as parents, must help our kids see the bright side of every situation, and they will in turn attract friends with similar views. I am sure we all agree that we want our children talking and e-mailing about the good stuff, not the bad.

For our children to be the company that other happy children will desire, they must think positive. There are many days that I can find my share of things to complain about, but I hold back and try to express the happier things. This is true even on days when good things aren't very apparent. The way children look at their day will impact on their happiness and their success. When we feel happy, we do well. When we are upset or distraught it is hard to concentrate, let alone learn.

We are living in a material world where appearance seems to be most important. But the truth is that after an initial view from the outside, what really matters and counts is attitude and vision. Help your child feel good about him- or herself.

WAYS TO BOOST YOUR CHILD'S SELF-ESTEEM

- Tell them you love them each day.
- Spend some one-on-one time with your child frequently.
- Acknowledge things they do well.
- Give your child opportunities to make choices, overcome little challenges, and experience success.
- Praise your child for things well done.
- Avoid comparing your children to others or using names that belittle a child when you are upset.

When Eric, 15, meets John, they hit it off and become instant friends. Over time, being with Eric becomes risky—he always wants to do daredevil things, including harassing neighbors and trashing their lawns. Unless everyone is doing what he wants to do, Eric is not happy. Just hanging out, seeing a movie, or talking is never good enough, and it always ends with Eric and John nagging each other, and then Eric going home mad. Trying to keep the friendship is not worth the possible consequences faced from hanging out with Eric. It takes a while, but with the help of his family, John realizes that having a friend like Eric isn't safe or even fun. Does your child know when to walk away from a friend with destructive behaviors, or one who just plain makes them unhappy?

Even though we want our children to look on the bright side of life, it is essential that we as parents help them see that there are times when they need to cut their losses and walk away. The key to successful parenting is helping your child recognize these times and understand the difference between quitting and changing paths.

Justin, 11, runs up to people in the school hallway and burps in their face or puts his bottom on them, passes gas, and then laughs hysterically. The majority of the sixth graders that go to school with Justin find him childish, rude, and repulsive. Over time, Justin comes home and complains to his mom that he isn't invited to a lot of the parties. Justin's mom responds, "Don't worry about those kids that don't invite you. Just ignore them." When Justin exhibits this behavior at home, his parents laugh it off as boy stuff. Justin's parents need to explain to him that at a certain age, bodily functions and noises are private and definitely should never be the topic of discussion or displayed publicly. Justin needs a talk about manners and respecting others. Many times our children need us to point out behaviors that isolate them from others.

Diana, 13, and Kimberly have been friends since kindergarten. They have always been good students and involved in the same clubs and activities. Diana receives the special honor roll award for her outstanding academic achievement and has a science fair project that won first prize and a hundred dollar gift certificate. Kimberly starts to have other girls gang up on Diana and shut her out of a seat at their lunch table and invitations to weekend events, such as a trip to the movies or a get-together at someone's house. Diana is crushed and asks her mom to talk to Kimberly's mom to find out why Kimberly is trying to get everyone to hate her. Diana's mom doesn't know what to do and secretly cries because of her daughter's unhappiness. Diana's mother needs to sit down and explain the concept of jealousy and tell Diana that she is very proud of her, but, unfortunately, sometimes young girls can't control their feelings of jealousy and lash out at others, even their own friends. Unless the situation escalates and Diana's parents feel that she is being bullied or harassed, they need to let Diana work out this situation with her friend and decide if it is time to make new friends.

Sometimes the pressure from other children can lead children to purposely performing poorly in school. This "dumbing down" to fit in doesn't help children and just leads to additional problems from declining grades. This type of behavior is rather common among adolescents, and parents should discuss this with their children to avoid this potentially detrimental reaction.

Unkind behavior is certainly hurtful and we must remind our children not to follow in the footsteps of those who hurt them. There is a happy balance where children can defend themselves and separate themselves from others without resorting to similar or rude behavior. Sharing stories about how we as parents, when we were younger, have experienced some of the things our children are going through will help them realize that they are not alone and will survive the hurt and pain.

Don't dismiss their feelings, but help them realize that some children do not understand about true friendship and the importance of kindness. Remind them of their strengths and why they are so special and unique. Tell them you are proud of them and that it is often difficult for their peers to see their special gifts and talents in order to appreciate them and not envy them.

Talk about jealousy and help your children overcome the temptation to display envy. Remind them there will always be others who have something they don't. Feelings of jealousy come from feelings of insecurity. Don't compare your children to others and don't let them compare themselves to others. There will always be someone who can run faster, achieve a little more, or get invited to a few more parties.

Not being the best at a particular thing doesn't make you less than anyone else. Help your children feel good about who they are and build their self-esteem to avoid falling in a jealousy trap. Children who are constantly envious of others aren't able to build and sustain friendships.

ACTIVITY AND CONVERSATION STARTERS

- Make a list of blessings or things to be thankful for with your child.
- Make a list of things your child/student wants to improve with some suggestions to work toward the goal.
- Make a list of things you are proud of in regard to your child or student.

CONVERSATION STARTERS

- I remember a time I felt jealous and did . . .
- When I start to feel jealous, I change my thoughts to something else like . . .
- What activity can we put you in to take your mind off things you wish you had or did better? Read a book? Ride your bike?

7

WELL SAID, LADIES AND GENTLEMEN!

Joshua, 12, returns home from school. "Do you have any homework?" asks Joshua's mother. "Yeah!" he answers. "How was your school day?" He responds, "It sucked," as he pushes and trips his little brother, Alex. Joshua's mother just shrugs her shoulders and says, "Don't use that kind of language, and leave your brother alone." She hasn't properly set the standard for acceptable manners in terms of speaking and interacting with others. She needs to correct the slang and teach Joshua to use proper words to respond. The treatment of the younger sibling should be addressed and proper behavior modeled and expected. Simply telling Joshua to leave his younger brother alone won't teach him how to treat others or how to respond appropriately to adults.

Being able to verbally communicate effectively with others is essential in school and life. Parents should help children learn how to express themselves in all types of situations. Kids need to feel comfortable talking with other kids and adults. They must think about what they are trying to say, and their feelings, and then relax and speak.

Children must practice politeness and respect when they are asking questions, responding to requests, and making requests. If your child seems nervous and apprehensive about interacting with others, provide opportunities to practice. If you go to a store to buy something your child wants or needs, let them ask for assistance in locating the item and size or quantity. Help them feel comfortable talking with others. This will make it easier when they have to make requests and you aren't with them.

You have probably met children who hide behind their parents when others approach. They may even beg a parent to ask the question or deliver a message. Certainly there are shy children, but parents must help them feel at ease with others. Even if they are reluctant, make your children ask for things they want or need. Over time, speaking out will become easy and not be a source of stress.

Public speaking and communication are not always taught in school. Parents should be sure they give their child the gift of clear communication and clear speaking skills. Practice your comfort level with speaking in all types of environments. There are ten simple rules parents and educators can use to help children improve their communication skills.

Rule 1. Make people feel understood by being understanding, sympathetic, and listening. Successful communication means listening to others and considering their feelings and thoughts. Ask your child to repeat to you what they think you said. This will help you see how well your child listens during a conversation.

Rule 2. Be energetic in your delivery when speaking. Slow down for a dramatic point and speed up to show excitement. Don't argue about things. Give your opinion but be open to the different ideas of others. Show facial expression as you speak. Smile when talking about something pleasant and let your face show other emotions as you tell about an event or activity. Whatever your movements, they should have purpose.

Rule 3. Think before speaking and show genuine caring for the people you are talking with. If you are concerned about the people you're speaking with, they'll know it and respond more freely.

Rule 4. Think about what you want to say and organize your thoughts.

Rule 5. Tell your own story somewhere in the presentation. You want to help the audience link emotionally with what you are talking about, and the personal experience does that. With almost any topic you might choose, you have at least one "war story" to relate to the topic. When you tell the story, simply start at the beginning and move chronologically through the narrative, including answers to the "W" questions: who, what, when, why, and where. Look at the audience you are speaking to. Maintain good eye contact when you are speaking to be clear, as well as commanding immediate attention.

Rule 6. Be exciting.

Rule 7. Consider using a touch of humor when you speak to people. You are not becoming a comedian but rather lightening up a serious talk so that people will be more accepting and interested in your ideas. Humor will help you to be perceived as an amiable person.

Rule 8. Don't interrupt others.

Rule 9. Engage as many of your senses as you can during a conversation. The audience's interest in the discussion will remain higher.

Rule 10. Teach by example. Practice the art of conversation and role play the right way to hold a conversation.

Speaking politely can be taught and practiced, but sincerity must be genuine. Too often children today don't appreciate the things they have and don't realize just how fortunate they really are. We blame the media, our selfish culture, and even the grandparents. However unknowingly, parents are to blame by indulging children with everything they want but really don't necessarily need, earn, or deserve. Failing to set limits and not fostering responsibility with chores is the parents' fault. Are your children appreciative of the things you buy them? Parents can and should strive to develop a habit of being grateful, appreciating what they have, thanking others for gifts, acknowledging kind acts, understanding limits, and respecting luxuries!

Remind children to be grateful for their belongings and those special people in their lives. Thank yous are too few and too far between. Have your children write thank you cards for birthday and other special occasion gifts. Discuss people that are less fortunate. Remind your children that some children go to bed hungry. Let them make a personal donation to someone less fortunate. A warm home and stocked kitchen isn't true for everyone. Make sure they always say please and thank you, and that you, the parent, model it as well.

Teach children that money doesn't grow on trees. Help them understand that money is earned from hard work and should be spent wisely. Besides raising children that become spoiled and unappreciative, we may be setting our children up for poor spending habits that lead to severe financial difficulties that last a lifetime. The fastest growing bankruptcy rate is in adults under twenty-five.

Show your child the difference between what they want and what they really need. In both children and adults, working hard for things makes them feel better about receiving them. What children really need and remember most is time spent with family and family values.

ACTIVITY AND CONVERSATION STARTERS

With your child make a list of needs and wants.

CONVERSATION STARTERS

- Tell me a story.
- Do you know any jokes?
- Explain a time when . . .

8

PLEASE AND THANK YOU!

Samantha, 9, knows everything and has everything. Regardless of what a student has for show-and-tell, she always has something better and more exciting. She has an unfortunate tendency to think she is better than everyone, which can cause other students to feel as if they are lower than her or have less than her. She is spoiled as an only child. Her parents don't realize that by overindulging their daughter, they are not teaching her how to interact with others, therefore making her feel superior to all her peers. Every time her class has open discussions, she interrupts her peers and never raises her hand. The teacher often tells Samantha to raise her hand or wait her turn, but Samantha doesn't understand why. Samantha's parents need to remind her to wait her turn and hear what others have to say.

Just as adults don't like being around other adults with bad manners, children feel the same way. Children with bad manners, who are rude and impolite rarely make and keep friends. The most important way to teach good manners is to model them. If you want your children to say "please" and "thank you," be sure that those words are routinely used in your life or are a routine part of your vocabulary.

The best person to teach manners is you, the parent, because children will follow your example. When you're out and about, point out people with good behavior and point out people with poor behavior. When you see a child acting appropriately, discuss it with your child and explain how nice it is. Openly commend that child and the parent.

On the other hand, when you see a child exhibit inappropriate or rude behavior, ask your child whether he or she would want to hang around with someone like that. When your child displays rude behavior, try not to yell, scream, or punish him or her harshly. The best way to reduce rude behavior is to take away privileges or toys.

When your child shows polite behavior, reward him or her with special privileges. Sitting around the dinner table is a great way to talk about manners. The way you eat tells a lot about you. Start off with proper use of a fork and knife. Show your children how to cut their steak, chew with their mouth closed, put their napkin in their lap, and serve themselves the amount they will be able to eat.

Help them to try new things and they may surprise you and say, "Please give me some more" when they love it and, "No thank you" when they don't care for something. Making faces, showing disgust, taking huge portions that they will not finish, and refusing to try something must not be allowed. When your child masters the art of eating, reward them by going to a restaurant of their choice. Explain that because of their wonderful manners and eating skills, they get to dine out in public and make you proud.

Teaching your child to have good manners does not happen overnight. Manners must be expected, discussed, and practiced before they become lifelong habits. Most parents correct their children when they pick their noses, pass gas, or bite their nails. Besides these obvious behaviors, there are many others that make a child likable and someone that others want to be around.

We all have likes and dislikes, but today we see more and more children refusing to take part in an activity, then saying I don't want to or I hate that. Hate should be considered one of the four-letter words that is unacceptable under all circumstances. In my own home, I follow the advice of my older sister, who has a toddler, school-age child, and teenager. She always told her children they were not allowed to say the word hate, but when they didn't like something they were taught to say I don't care for that. It is quite impressive when I offer my two-year-old nephew some raisins and he says, "No thanks, I don't care for them."

Hate is a word for a strong feeling of negativity, usually accompanied by bad wishes and thoughts. There is never a reason to allow our children to hate. There may be times a child doesn't like something, like a certain food or a certain book, a certain game, or in extreme cases, a certain someone. Let them know it's okay not to care for something, but don't ever allow hate to enter your home or, even worse, your child.

Imagine your child is in school and meets a friend who tells your child that he or she is taking karate and will soon be entering a contest. Now imagine your child saying "I hate karate." Do you really think this friendship is going to blossom or last? Your child doesn't have to enjoy everything that everyone else does. In order to have friends you have to respect others' likes and dislikes.

Sometimes kids have habits that they think are funny but are really annoying to others. For example, there are kids who every time they see another kid, they whack them in the back or pull their hair. They think it's cute, but most of the other children try their best to avoid them, and talk about them when they're not around. Take notice of the behaviors your child displays and be certain he or she doesn't have any behaviors that could be turning kids off to your child. You may also wish to address this blatant cry for attention.

Learning to wait their turn and not interrupting other people when they are speaking is an important social skill. No one can be heard if there are too many voices at once. Gently tell your child to wait until someone is finished speaking, and then ask his or her question. This goes hand in hand with practice, which we as parents know is a virtue.

Be sure to give your child your full attention when you are done speaking so as to reinforce the positive behavior of waiting his or her turn. While your child is patiently waiting, hold his or her hand or put your arm around your child to let him or her know you are aware of their presence.

Norman, 11, has always been a little overweight compared to other children his own age. When he enters sixth grade, being a little bit overweight seems to be as bad as having the plague. A certain group of girls bangs on the desk and says, "Here comes the elephant" as Norman walks by. Another boy says, "Do you have to have your uniform special ordered because there is no way they have them that big?" Another boy says, "Can you tell me where fat kids buy their clothes, so if I ever meet anyone as fat as you I can tell them where to shop?" Norman, over time tries to become invisible in the classroom and stays away from his peers as much as possible. He starts to hold his head down, doesn't seem to care about himself, and rarely smiles.

Norman's parents need to open the lines of communication with their son and pry into why Norman has become unhappy and less social. Norman's parents need to help him see that name-calling is never appropriate, and he needs to let it go in one ear and out the other. If Norman's weight seems to be the cause of his unhappiness, guiding him to healthier meal choices and some light exercise is a healthy option, which can help him to feel better. At age eleven, some children are entering puberty and their body image, and how others see them, is an important part of how they see themselves.

We must help our children see that everyone is different and we all have strengths and weaknesses. No one enjoys having their weaknesses pointed out, ridiculed, or focused on. It is essential in your list of manners that you teach your children that name calling is unacceptable, even if it's meant to be a joke.

Be sure that you don't tease or call names with other family members and friends in jest. Remember, children model the behavior of the environment in which they live. Don't let the environment be one of sarcasm, teasing, or hurtful behaviors. This may sound odd to even mention because we all know how to behave in front of our children. Our children are like little sponges just waiting to absorb any information they may overhear, such as your phone conversations with other adults; everything they hear is saved and becomes future ammunition.

We have all heard of the hearty greeting used often in Texas—"Howdy partner." Greeting should not be something that we read about in Southern traditions, rather it should be something that we practice every day with the people with whom we interact. I am certainly not advocating teaching your children to go up to strangers and say "hello."

In today's world, we must teach our children how to protect themselves from strangers and, unfortunately, we must protect them from child predators and the horrible acts we hear about too often on the evening news. However, on a given day our children see many people that they should greet to show respect. Your child should greet any person that may enter your home. For example, when a family member comes over, children should be taught to greet them with a hello and minimally how are you. Be sure to discuss proper titles and the level of formality you expect.

Sometimes young children call close friends aunt and uncle as a sign of respect, even when there is no blood relationship. Discuss whether children should call adults by their first names, or use Mr. and Mrs. Remind them to greet their teachers and other adults in the school, such as the principal, school nurse, or counselor. When speaking to adults, a smile and a glance of the eye go a long way.

My family has been in the restaurant business for many years. My father has often encouraged me to write an article about manners. He constantly grumbles that children today just don't say "Please" and "Thank you" anymore. And then he laughs a little because, come to think of it, most adults don't either. When I help out on the weekends from time to time, he constantly reminds me to say goodnight and thank you as customers leave the restaurant. If you want your children to say please and thank you, they must hear it from you over and over again.

Imagine if our spouses and children said please and thank you every time we did something for them. I personally would love to hear my husband say, "Thanks for cleaning my clothes and cooking this wonderful dinner." I won't hold my breath for this to happen, but I certainly can model and practice please and thank you to the point where they become frequently used words in my children's vocabulary. Of course we don't want to raise habitual robots—so they should understand the meaning.

Meals are often seen as celebrations and times where families and friends can interact. Table manners are the perfect opportunity to help your child learn manners. In school, lunch manners are important and help kids be invited to sit with friends. Teachers can use lunchtime to watch students interact with others.

Children must learn how to cut food and the proper use of utensils. Discuss chewing with your mouth closed and not stuffing your mouth full of food, because it looks gross and they could choke. Kids shouldn't comment about the food being served or what others are eating. Remind them to not pick their teeth, reach across the table, and to use a napkin. And of course, never speak with your mouth full.

Remember, children who consistently use proper table manners have had a lot of practice. They use their utensils properly each time they eat. When children are taught the right way to do something it becomes a habit that they are likely to continue even when you aren't present.

When you are helping them to form these polite habits be sure to remind them that good table manners are part of being considerate. They certainly wouldn't want to have a meal while watching someone mutilate food with a knife, fork, or spoon. They also wouldn't like to see someone with food hanging out of his or her mouth while they are dining. Being respectful that others are eating is an essential part of table manners and treating others. One of my personal favorite sayings is, "You are known by the way you eat!"

ACTIVITY AND CONVERSATION STARTERS

Make a list of the ten most important table manners and rank them in order of importance.

To help talk about manners:

- Who is the most polite person you know?
- Tell me about a time when you witnessed someone who was rude or impolite.
- How should you address your teacher? The principal? Your family members? Your friends' parents?

9

PARENT SENSE

After reading this book, you should feel better about how to follow your kids' social life and decide what kind of advice to offer. Parents who take a deep interest in their kids' social interactions will help their children succeed in all aspects of their lives. Sometimes just talking about your child's experiences and reminding them they can just walk away when someone is mean to them is all you need to do. Other times you must step in and assist. Today, helping your child choose friends and helping your child not choose certain others is essential to his or her overall development. In today's world there will always be people and issues to deal with, be sure you are knowledgeable and assist your child to address them appropriately.

Now that you have read my book I hope I have opened some doors for you to help you understand and cope with the subject of bullying. I have tried to show common yet complex issues relating to this real-life problem facing our children and young adults today and given you some proven strategies to prevent and conquer it. However, no matter how many books we read and examples we study, I want to state clearly that the best solution to this problem is you, the parent. You know your child best. Only you are able to look at your child and know when he or she is out of sorts, sad, pressured, or just not really him- or herself. Never hesitate to act on your own instincts, ask questions and share your thoughts and advice.

If we close our eyes to these situations they really don't go away; in fact, they grow into bigger and more serious problems. Even situations that may seem insignificant to you can pose a danger to your child. Learn to differentiate between a joke and bullying. Don't let harmful acts repeat themselves. Step in from the beginning and nip the problem in the bud before your child really needs help. Teach your child correct and proper behavior. Let your child emulate you in the manner he or she can judge who to associate with and who not to associate with.

Our children learn what we teach and preach to them. We need to know when to step in and when to let them handle the situation themselves. We need to know their teachers well and their friends and so-called friends even better. If there is a gap in communication, close it. Listen to your child with compassion and understanding, and never hesitate to give an honest and unbiased opinion. Work together as a team. "United we stand, divided we fall" works for the nation, why not for your family?

Love and respect are emotions that go hand in hand in a two-way street and are earned by hard work, patience, and the ability to give of one's self. There is no advice better than your own. Along with love and understanding, we teach our children by correcting and explaining. We paint the picture of life, which teaches right from wrong and what proper and improper behavior is.

When children learn this concept they grow smarter and develop the ability to make wiser choices in their own lives. This leads them to make the best choices of who they want to associate with and who they should avoid. Thus, they come across fewer problems and fewer problematic situations. Don't be afraid to correct and teach, you will bring out the best in your children. Additionally, they will grow up to be better and stronger adults, mentally and physically ready to cope with whatever life brings.

I hope through my writing I have helped you in some way turn the world of a child into a better, softer, and more fun place to live. The family is the heart and soul of life. We must protect and keep it sacred for the generations to come by encouraging peace, love, and happiness for all.

Talk with your child about school each day. These conversations often serve as catalysts to open discussions that may prevent unnecessary teasing or bullying. My wish is for every parent to build relationships that help keep parents "in" when children leave them "out." No child should suffer in silence and no parent should regret not stepping in. Make sure that a single day doesn't go by without sending the message that you are there and always ready to listen. Leave messages on your child's desk or bed to initiate conversations, mend issues, reinforce that things will get better, and simply remind them of your love.

Finally, remember that you are your child's first and best teacher. The lessons they learn from you not only enlighten their minds, but also form their character. Teachers must keep in mind that the best way to serve their students is to help parents understand their role and importance in forming children's lives.

ABOUT THE AUTHOR

Meline Kevorkian, EdD, is associate dean for master's and educational specialist programs for the Fischler School of Education and Human Services at Nova Southeastern University. She is also a columnist at the *Miami Herald,* and her experience includes teaching and administrative positions in both public and private schools from preschool through the university level. She is the mother of two and author of *Six Secrets for Parents to Help Their Kids Achieve in School* (Rowman & Littlefield Education, 2005).

In my 37 years as a journalist, I have seen many great teams, athletes, and coaches. I have found the ones that stand together and encourage each other more often than not come out on top. No matter what the score is at the end of the day, they walk away from the experience a better person. Never underestimate the power to be persuasive through kindness and good word. The fact of the matter is it takes the same amount of time and energy with little result to be a bully or just plain mean. Teaching our children to respect one another is one of our biggest challenges and probably the one we spend the least amount of time on. That is why the most effective way to enlighten our children is through example, teaching them through our own behavior how to be kind to the cashier at the grocery store or the homeless man on the street. It is from witnessing these displays of kindness that out children learn most.

—Tony Segreto